HUMAN BODY SYSTEMS

WHAT IS THE RESPIRATORY SYSTEM?

KENG XIONG

childsworld.com

The Child's World®
childsworld.com

Published by The Child's World®
800-599-READ · www.childsworld.com

Photography Credits
Photographs ©: Shutterstock Images, cover (main), cover
(icon), 1 (main), 1 (icon), 3, 5, 7, 9, 11, 13, 16, 17, 18–19, 20, 22;
Sebastian Kaulitzki/Shutterstock Images, 10; Drazen
Zigic/Shutterstock Images, 14–15; Design elements from
Shutterstock Images

ISBN Information
9781503871335 (Reinforced Library Binding)
9781503871625 (Portable Document Format)
9781503872868 (Online Multi-user eBook)
9781503874107 (Electronic Publication)

LCCN 2024951067

Printed in the United States of America

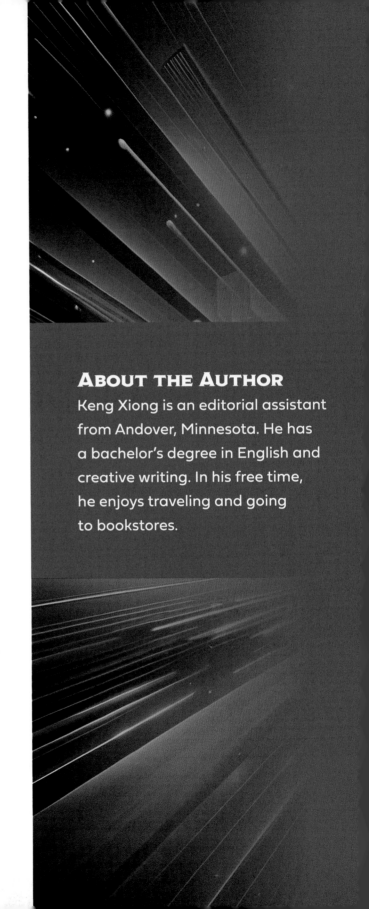

ABOUT THE AUTHOR
Keng Xiong is an editorial assistant
from Andover, Minnesota. He has
a bachelor's degree in English and
creative writing. In his free time,
he enjoys traveling and going
to bookstores.

TABLE OF CONTENTS

TAKING A DEEP BREATH

It is the final race of Lucas's school swim meet. He balances himself on the diving block. He takes a deep breath. Then he counts to three and breathes out. This calms him down.

A buzzer blares to signal the start of the race. Lucas dives into the water. His muscles work hard. His arms slice through the water. His legs kick him forward. He takes quick gulps of air when he can. Swimming is hard. But he loves the feeling of the water. He looks ahead. The end of the race is in sight.

Swimming raises a person's heart and breathing rates.

Lucas reaches the other end of the pool. He pulls himself onto the pool's edge. His chest rises and falls with his fast breathing. His heart thumps. He looks at the scoreboard and smiles. He got first place! He could not have done it without his respiratory system.

The respiratory system is an important part of the human body. It takes in a gas called oxygen from the air. This happens when a person breathes in, or inhales. Body parts need oxygen to function. The body produces another gas called carbon dioxide as waste. The respiratory system releases this waste when a person breathes out, or exhales. The cycle of breathing keeps the body working properly.

The air contains many gases besides oxygen, such as nitrogen and argon.

Organs of the respiratory system include the nose, mouth, airways, and lungs. These parts allow people to breathe air. It is important to take care of the respiratory system. People need a constant supply of air to survive.

CHAPTER 2

HOW BREATHING WORKS

The respiratory cycle begins when a person inhales. Air enters the body through the nose or mouth. The nose helps warm and moisten the air. This happens as air moves over **tissue** filled with blood vessels. This makes the air less likely to irritate parts deeper inside the system.

The nostrils are the two openings in a person's nose.

Cilia are so small that they cannot be seen with the naked eye.

JAMES HARDY

On June 11, 1963, Dr. James Hardy and his team performed the world's first successful human lung transplant. The patient lived for 18 days. Doctors later found better ways to transplant lungs. More than 2,700 lung transplants were performed in the United States in 2022. About half the people who receive lung transplants live for another 5 years.

The air travels into the throat. This area contains the voice box and windpipe. The voice box shakes as air passes over it. This allows people to talk. Air continues into the windpipe. The windpipe contains mucus (MYOO-kus) and cilia (SIL-ee-yuh). Mucus is a sticky substance. It helps trap **particles** such as dust or harmful **germs**. It also helps moisten inhaled air. Cilia are small, hairlike structures. They push invading substances out of the respiratory system.

Air then travels into the airways. Large tubes branch out into thinner tubes. They lead to large organs called lungs. Lungs contain about 150 million tiny air sacs. These sacs are called alveoli (al-VEE-oh-lye). Alveoli are connected to blood vessels.

Oxygen from the air enters the blood through the alveoli. The blood then carries the oxygen throughout the body. Meanwhile, carbon dioxide from the blood goes into the alveoli. The waste gas then travels out of the body the same way the air came in.

Surrounding the respiratory system is the thorax. This region of the body protects the lungs and heart. It is made of muscles and bones. Below the thorax is the diaphragm (DYE-uh-fram). This large muscle helps with breathing. The diaphragm pulls down to suck in air. It relaxes to push out a person's breath.

PARTS OF THE RESPIRATORY SYSTEM

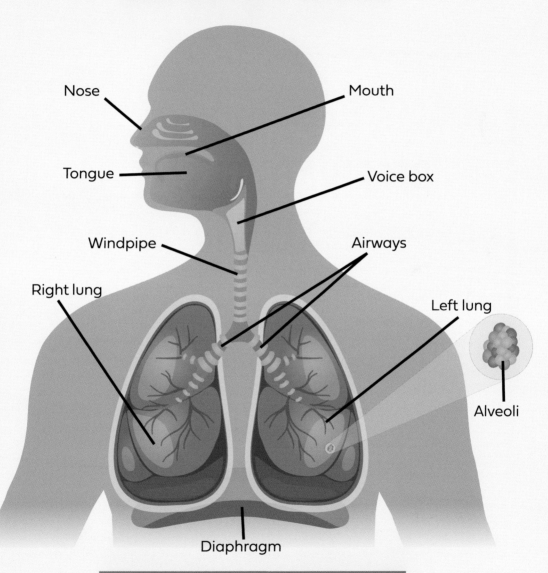

Nose

Mouth

Tongue

Voice box

Windpipe

Airways

Right lung

Left lung

Alveoli

Diaphragm

This diagram displays the major parts of the respiratory system and how they are connected to each other in the body.

KEEPING THE RESPIRATORY SYSTEM STRONG

A strong respiratory system helps the body take in oxygen and release carbon dioxide. The body relies on the constant exchange of these gases. Problems with the respiratory system can disrupt the body's functions.

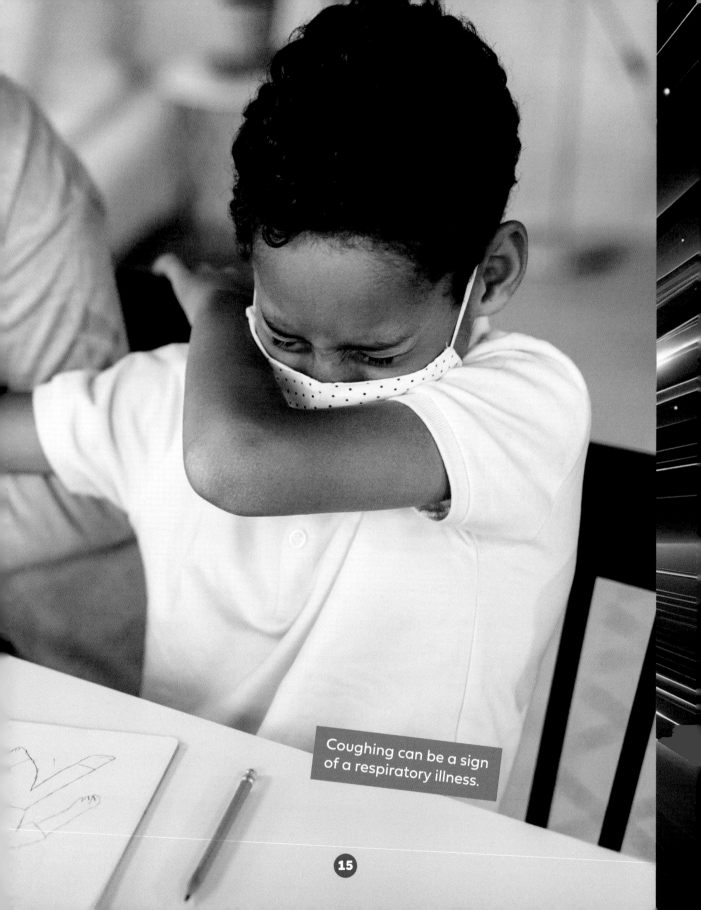

Coughing can be a sign of a respiratory illness.

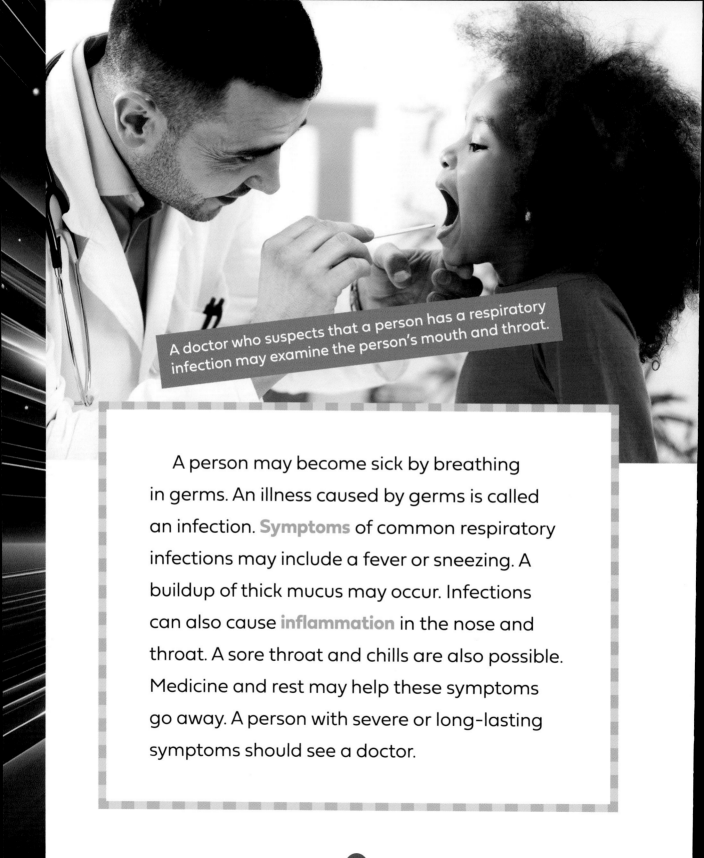

A doctor who suspects that a person has a respiratory infection may examine the person's mouth and throat.

A person may become sick by breathing in germs. An illness caused by germs is called an infection. **Symptoms** of common respiratory infections may include a fever or sneezing. A buildup of thick mucus may occur. Infections can also cause **inflammation** in the nose and throat. A sore throat and chills are also possible. Medicine and rest may help these symptoms go away. A person with severe or long-lasting symptoms should see a doctor.

For handwashing to be effective, people should use soap and wash their hands for at least 20 seconds.

Germs can spread in many ways. Germs that cause respiratory illnesses often spread as particles in the air. People can get sick by breathing in these particles. Sometimes germs settle on surfaces such as tables. Washing hands helps reduce the spread of these germs. So does avoiding close contact with other people.

The respiratory system can have other problems not caused by illness. Suffocation happens when a person cannot get air. Suffocation is very dangerous. A lack of oxygen to the lungs or brain can lead to death.

Choking happens when something gets stuck in a person's windpipe. Food in the windpipe is a common cause of choking. Eating slowly can reduce the chance of choking.

Drowning happens when a person suffocates in water. The water blocks air from entering the lungs. Learning how to swim can reduce the chance of drowning.

Some people with asthma use inhalers. These devices allow people to breathe in medicine for their asthma.

ASTHMA
Asthma is one of the most common chronic diseases in children. Chronic diseases are long-lasting and must be treated over time. Asthma causes the airways to narrow. This can make it hard to breathe. There is no cure for asthma. But treatments can reduce a person's symptoms.

Running is one kind of exercise that can benefit the respiratory system.

There are many things a person can do for their respiratory system. Exercising helps keep the lungs and breathing muscles strong. Drinking water keeps the airways and lungs moist. People can avoid smoking to protect the respiratory system from damage over time. A person should talk to a doctor if they have concerns about their respiratory system.

WONDER MORE

Wondering About New Information

How much did you know about the respiratory system before reading this book? What new information did you learn? Write down three new facts that this book taught you. Was the new information surprising? Why or why not?

Wondering How It Matters

A strong respiratory system helps a person stay active. Problems with the respiratory system can affect a person's life. Do you or someone you know struggle with respiratory illness?

Wondering Why

The lungs are important organs in the respiratory system. Why do you think people are usually born with two lungs when they can often survive with only one? How might having one lung affect a person's life?

Ways to Keep Wondering

The respiratory system is one of many human body systems. After reading this book, what questions do you have about the respiratory system? What can you do to learn more about it?

FAST FACTS

- Body parts need oxygen in order to work properly.

- The respiratory system takes oxygen into the body. It also releases carbon dioxide.

- Air enters the lungs through the airways. Tiny air sacs in the lungs exchange oxygen and carbon dioxide in the blood.

- Things can go wrong with the respiratory system. Signs that something is wrong can include a fever, a buildup of mucus, and trouble breathing.

- A person can help keep their respiratory system strong by exercising and avoiding smoking. A person should talk to a doctor if they have concerns about their respiratory system.

BALLOON MODEL

1. Bend two bendable straws. Lay them next to each other with the bent ends in opposite directions. Tape the straws together at the unbent ends.

2. Next, tape two balloons to cover the straw openings at the bent ends. Make sure the balloons are tightly fixed to the straws.

3. Inflate the balloons by blowing into the straws.

4. Answer the following questions by yourself or with a partner: What organs do the straws and balloons represent? How does this model represent the function of the respiratory system?

GLOSSARY

germs (JERMZ) Germs are very small living things or viruses that can cause disease. Nose hairs trap germs to stop them from entering the body.

inflammation (in-fluh-MAY-shun) Inflammation is a process in which the body defends itself from a threat by swelling, warming, and performing other functions. Inflammation can occur when someone is sick with a respiratory illness.

organs (OR-gunz) Organs are collections of cells and tissues that work together to do a task. The lungs and windpipe are important organs in the respiratory system.

particles (PAR-tih-kullz) Particles are tiny parts of something. The air is full of particles that people breathe in.

symptoms (SIMP-tumz) Symptoms are signs of a medical condition. Someone may develop respiratory symptoms if they inhale harmful germs.

tissue (TIH-shyoo) Tissue is a group of similar cells that work together. Tissue makes up parts of the windpipe and lungs.

transplant (TRANZ-plant) A transplant is a medical operation in which a body part is moved from its original location to a new one. The first successful human lung transplant happened in 1963.

Find Out More

In the Library

An, Priscilla. *Mindfulness While Playing Sports*. Parker, CO: The Child's World, 2024.

Schuh, Mari. *Riley's Remarkable Respiratory System*. Minneapolis, MN: Jump!, 2022.

Xiong, Keng. *What Is the Circulatory System?* Parker, CO: The Child's World, 2026.

On the Web

Visit our website for links about the respiratory system:

childsworld.com/links

Note to Parents, Caregivers, Teachers, and Librarians: We routinely verify our web links to make sure they are safe and active sites. So encourage your readers to check them out!

Index